The Stones *of* Strasbourg

& Other Poems

The Stones *of* Strasbourg *& Other Poems*

H. R. Stoneback

Codhill Press
New Paltz, New York

Codhill books are published
by David Appelbaum for Codhill Press

First Edition

Book and cover design by Alicia Fox

Library of Congress Cataloging-in-Publication Data
Stoneback, H. R. (Harry Robert), 1941–
[Poems. Selections]
The stones of Strasbourg & other poems / H. R. Stoneback. —First edition.
pages; cm
ISBN 1-930337-85-X (alk. paper)
I. Title.

PS3569.T6436A6 2015
811'.54—dc23

2015012520

For Maître d'oeuvre Erwin von Steinbach & Sabina von Steinbach—
architects, builders, sculptors: The Strasbourg Cathedral

Contents

THE STONES OF STRASBOURG

THE STONES OF STRASBOURG
I. Family History & Ancestral Myths

Gigantic and delicate marvel
Hugo on the Strasbourg Cathedral

Sublimely towering, wide-spreading tree of God
Goethe on the Strasbourg Cathedral

I heard the stories from early childhood
when I had no interest in genealogy
and *knew* I was the American Adam
rising singular, alone, from my native earth,

radically free to make and claim my own lineage.
When my 105-year-old great grandmother
told stories in the 1950s of witnessing
troop movements in the Battle of Gettysburg,

hearing the guns in the distance, I barely
listened, my mind hearing Elvis, my rock-
a-billy heart tuned to another rhythm—
cool, clean, all present and future. No dim

echoes of the dead past allowed in my kid-world.
Still I heard the tales, mostly told by great-
aunts, schoolteachers and storytellers
in their 90s. My father and mother,

children of the Roaring 20s and The Great
Depression, never repeated the stories.
One grandmother, a Brownback before she
was a Stoneback, told how our people founded

Germantown in the 1600s and built Philadelphia.
One time she said there was no shame in Prussian
warrior Catholic conservative blood because they
hated Hitler as much as they hated the Communists

and besides, that Prussian noble blood had long ago
been tempered by English and Scottish and our main
Pennsylvania Dutch line, moderate and Rittenhouse.
She told me this sitting on a bench in

Rittenhouse Square, in downtown Philly, right
before we went to John Wanamaker's
for lunch and the grand organ recital.
That was the day she said: "Your grandfather

that you never saw socialized with John
Wanamaker." And then she said: "That organ
is worthy of a great cathedral like
the one in Strasbourg, France that your ancestor

Erwin von Steinbach built. Some day you must see
it—the finest building in all Europe."
I know that was the first time I ever heard
the name *von Steinbach* but I can't recall

what else she said or if I asked questions.
When she talked about family history
it felt like fairy tales or ancient myths
to me, raised in poverty, in a row-house

slum in Camden. She had fallen some
from a great height, my parents fell faster
and farther, and I was starting from the bottom.
The other time I'm sure I heard the Steinbach

name as a kid was when my Great-Aunt Edie
came for her annual Christmas visit to our
slum-home, spent the whole time in a rocking
chair by the window with the heavy curtains

drawn to shut out the vicious street outside.
I think it was on the Christmas Eve when
the guy two doors down shot his wife, killed her—
we heard screams, shots, our street was blocked off,

sirens, lights flashing, more gunshots while the cops
ran him down outside our door: Christmas-music,
Camden-style—that's when Aunt Edie said: "Once upon
a time Stonebacks were important in the great

world when they worked in the best places. Makers,
builders. Your Steinbach forebear was the master-builder
and architect of the most magnificent
structure on this earth—in a place called Strasbourg

from which we fled long ago. And his daughter,
a sculptor, was the first great female artist
of Europe. That was long ago." Another
fairy tale, while next door the neighbors washed

blood from their front steps with buckets of water
as cop-cars and ambulances screamed into the night.
These stories rarely heard from my old people
were never repeated by my parents even

as desperate assertions of family pride,
for they were god-children of the Modern,
flapper and jazz musician, both poets—
at first. I may have heard old tales I forget

but I recall old things only when they are vividly
connected with places and events that surround
and evoke them, like great organs played
in vast spaces, like murder at the front door.

Later, when I discovered history
at last, almost too late to ask anybody
anything, I remembered vague tales
of haunted cathedrals, a Lady in White,

a blinded clock-maker, legions of ghost-masons
marching at midnight with builder's tools.
But then, as a boy, I believe I forgot old
tales as soon as they were told and I connected

nothing from the past with the unreasonable
love of stone that pervaded my childhood.
It may be that the word *Strasbourg* was inscribed
deep beneath consciousness, behind my increasing

book-knowing, imprinted somewhere in the undersong
of my boyish growing sense of worldhood.
But I do not *know* that—I only know
I had a haunted sense of stone. I could

stay all day by the Delaware River,
studying rocks and stones, piling them high,
building things unknown, knowing only I must
build higher and higher. A juvenile

delinquent gang-member in those sullen
streets of Camden, I knew I felt something
about stone my fellow gang-members could not
feel. They saw stone only as a weapon,

a device of destruction. When we watched
a tall crane and wrecking ball destroy a fine old
stone courthouse they cheered with savage delight.
I felt an infinite sadness and said nothing.

Walking the old historic streets of Philly,
I was bored by bricks but stopped in my tracks
by well-made stone chimneys or walls. When I first
saw a red sandstone doorway and steps I rubbed

my palms flat, outstretched over the smooth mauve
stone and wept and did not know why. Genetic
predisposition, I reckon. Maybe that's why
my older sister got a PhD in Geology.

I did not take everything for granite.
On my mother's side, a long line of Pennsylvania
Dutch builders of stone walls and stone barns on
certain lanes in Lancaster County which still

move me far and deep beyond the historical
knowledge that my ancestors built them.
They farmed for centuries around Bird-in-Hand,
Blue Ball, Paradise. First settlers of *Strasburg*.

Strasbourg! The great bell tolls, the *bourdon*
of history rings clear at last. On my mother's side,
lineage was never clear. As if everything began
in Lancaster County, her people autochthons

sprung from that fertile earth. No history
before Lancaster. She didn't know. Or
she wouldn't talk about it. When I visit
the Lancaster Farmers Market people

I've never seen stare at me, exclaim: "You've
come home!" But back beyond that earth—nothing:
My mother and her mother would not talk about it.
When, a grown man with a gnawing hunger for

a living sense of the past, I asked them
they both said nothing. Before he died, my father
whispered unclear tales of a wild Russian poet—
in some versions he was a Russian Jewish

poet and musician who frequented the Courts
of Europe, fell in love with the stones of Strasbourg
Cathedral and a girl from a famous stonemason family,
settled down next to the cathedral, then fled

with his bride to England when the religious wars
came, stayed there, then their children's children
pioneered the new Lancaster country.
My father did not have a name for this

mysterious Russian. The story did not fit
the sparse facts I had managed to compile
about my mother's family. After my
father died, I asked my mother about the wild

Russian troubadour in the family tree.
She said: "Your father was a poet. He made
things up." When I pressed her about the blank
spaces in the record, she finally said:

"Your grandmother was adopted. That's all
I can tell you. Sometimes the past is better
left alone. Some things are better not to know."
She said she did not know my grandmother's birth name,

knew only that her unknown father was a stonemason,
a poet. When I asked my grandmother about all this,
several times in her 90s, she always laughed
what we all called her wonderful Pennsylvania

Dutch laugh, then with a look of distance
said: "Some things are better not to know."
The last time, just before she died, she said: "In this
bloody century some things are better not to know."

At her funeral in the country Protestant Chapel,
I was thinking while the preacher talked *this*
is the first time I've ever seen my grandmother
in church when suddenly out of nowhere

the country preacher said: "Even a Jew
can go to heaven." At first I thought *why you*
redneck bastard then I realized these were
the last words spoken over *my grandmother*.

I looked at my mother. She looked away.
I thought—*She told that preacher what she would*
never tell me. Years later, just before she died,
I said *So Daddy's wild stories were all true.*

Truth or myth she said *Nobody knew all*
the facts. You must know grandma's secrecy sprang not
from shame but as a shield against the horror of history.
Again she said: *Some things are better not to know.*

The hell they are I thought but said nothing.
All is redeemed in knowledge: Strasbourg or
Strasburg. Incest or madness. Russian Jewish
poet singing in the family tree *O what*

is your name? Before the song is over
let me also proudly claim my Buddhist, Hindu,
Pagan, Chinese, Cherokee, my Greek
and Polynesian Aloha ancestors,

my Arctic and African family.
When Sparrow—my wife—and I eloped, fled
to Alabama to build a log house
in the wilderness, we told no family history.

One day in the woods she watched me placing
great stones for our cabin chimney and said:
"Promise me you'll take me to Strasbourg and Paris
someday." "OK. Paris, sure. But why *Strasbourg*?"

"I don't know. I had a strange dream last night
of a great cathedral you were building there
and I was carving figures on the façade.
Does Strasbourg have a cathedral? If so,

I want to see a picture to see if
it's like the cathedral in my dream."
In the few months since we met I'd never mentioned
Strasbourg or Erwin von Steinbach to her, barely

remembered all that then. When we finally saw
a picture in the library she said it was just like
in her dream. It may be part of this story that we learned
a few years later we were probably related

since our families had lived next to each other
and intermarried on the Virginia frontier
in the 1700s. It is part of this story
that later still when we went to France

the first time and Strasbourg the first time
she said: "We used to live here. We're home now."
She never played silly *past lives games*,
had never heard of eternal recurrence,

and I'd still never mentioned Steinbach to her because
I'd rarely thought of all that and had never checked
any sources. Finally, I told her the old family stories.
She cried and said: "Eternity is now."

We looked at the great spire soaring like God's tree.
"It always is but we can only say that in stone
and only when, beyond the bloody centuries, we're home."
We crossed to the *Kammerzell* for *Choucroute Alsacienne*.

II. Erwin von Steinbach 1244–1318

At your graveside again, holy Erwin, at and over the
eternal memorial of the life in you . . .

Goethe "Third Pilgrimage to Erwin's Grave, in July 1775"

Goethe [stands] in front of the memorial to Erwin von Steinbach.
In the storm of his feeling the veil of the historical cloud spread out
between them was torn apart. He saw the German work for the first
time once more, "working from the strong rough German soul."

Nietzsche *The Use and Abuse of History*

The next time we went to Strasbourg was two
years later. We were living in Paris that year.
I was visiting professor at the University of Paris
and sometimes I wrote out formal lectures,
which I had never done before (or since),
because I wanted to work in Eurosources and a few
French phrases and get them exact. I had planned

to stay home and write the rest of that week
because I had a big lecture coming up
billed as "Faulkner and the Southern Sense of the Past."
I was trying to weave some stuff from Nietzsche's
The Use and Abuse of History into my lecture.
I borrowed Foucault's copy of the Nietzsche from his
office—Foucault and Lacan were my colleagues then—

and read it twice. It was compelling to read,
but hard to remember exactly after
you'd read it. That was because while Nietzsche raged
against abstraction he gave the reader no images
to hold. He wanted to be but wasn't a poet.
That morning over coffee Sparrow said:
"Let's go to Strasbourg. I'll drive and you can read

your Nietzsche." It was hard to read him
in a moving car even when the country
you were riding through was so familiar
you didn't have to look at everything.
Something about the opacity of his prose,
its resistance to motion and destination.
"Look!" she said. We were still far from the city

when we saw the great cathedral rising

like an imminent space-launch vision,
like some God-rocket aimed for infinity.
We fixed it in our line of seeing around
every curve, over all the hills, holding
it from glimpse to glimpse until we arrived
in the center and parked in the shadow

of the vast red stone and again we were home.
We checked into our room at the *Maison*
Kammerzell happy with our half-timbered
Alsatian view and the incense aromas
from the restaurant downstairs. I only bumped
my head twice on the great low beam bisecting
our room before I got used to ducking.

It was easy for Sparrow to laugh because
she didn't have to duck. Still, we were lucky
to get a room since it was early December
and the *Marché de Noël* had started,
the Alsatian *Christkindelmärik*,
and all Europe knew Strasbourg was the true
"Capital of Christmas," home of the first

Christmas Tree and the largest oldest Christmas
Market, there at the key crossroads of France
and Germany. But since this is a *place-poem*
not a travel magazine article
I must say that we were there not for Christmas
cheer but to study Our Cathedral.
The reader may feel free to play some French

and German Christmas carols now, to look
at pictures of the immense Christmas Tree
taller than the one at Rockefeller Center, to know
the first recorded great tree was set up in the Strasbourg
Cathedral in the 1500s, to see all the lights, to smell
the wood fires burning in market food stalls
where chestnuts roasted and sausages were grilled,

to taste the hot bowl of *baeckeoffe* we bought and ate
in the light snow on the street, the subtle blend
of pork and lamb and beef with all the good
things that belong in a special Alsatian
stew that has simmered in a large pot
for three days, our stew cooled and seasoned by
snowflakes and carols choiring in the air

and we sang along. If you're not in the true
Strasbourg Christmas mood yet, dear reader,
have a cup of *vin chaud* with me, mulled wine,
and eat some *Christstollen* with us, laugh at
the powdered sugar on our lips and faces
from eating the traditional Christmas
fruit cake, a little too dry and not as good

as the authentic Dresden Christmas *stollen*,
not half as good as true Claxton fruitcake.
If you're exhausted now from shopping all
the stalls sprawled out around the Cathedral,
if you've bought your ornaments and handicrafts,
nutcrackers and Saint Nicholases, you may
come back to this poem now, which is not

a Christmas Market travel piece in that
old magazine in your doctor's office,
not a Facebook blog, not a Youtube video—
but a *place-poem, a cathedral-hymn.*
We slept sound in our 1500s beamed room
timber-chamber that slept us back toward the source,
toward the place we needed to be when we woke

and went out to do the homework we came
here to do, to study Our Cathedral, survey
the vertiginous verticalism
of the 466-foot tower, the dizzying spire
of what was the tallest building in the world
for more than two hundred years, taller than mere
Pyramids, and still the world's tallest building

intact from the Middle Ages. Our guide
seemed to think it a great mystery that the height
of the Cathedral exactly matched
the altitude above sea level of the ground
the building stood on. Maybe it is a *mystère*
for we cannot say by what divination
they measured the altitude. But the old

builders like Erwin von Steinbach knew many
things we have forgotten. And how, with such
massive spread and soar, did Steinbach's West Front
contain such intricate delicacy
in lacy openwork and tracery,
in details of crocketed cusps and curls,
all in consort with the operatic whole.

Goethe was right: this is a spreading God-tree.
Goethe was wrong: it's not the *strong rough German soul*
that these stones sing. That's very suspect, simple,
even for a young German Romantic.
All day, the Vosges red sandstone whispered nuance
to our eyes, susurration in color:
morning, noon, and twilight, dawn-pink, noon-red,

sunset-twilight-mauve, then dusk-purple, night-brown.
We went inside to study the interior,
not as much to study as to inhabit
the clean harmony of stained-glass nave-space,
to sit quietly and wish we were able to pray,
but we kept going out, then in, then out,
to stand in wordless stone glory of the West Front.

We spent some time in the *Musée de l'Oeuvre*
Notre-Dame next door, with its 14th-century
crenellated gable and the lovely spiral
staircase in the courtyard built when people
knew how to descend and ascend the stairs.
Since this had been the residence of *cathedral*
architects, the guide assured us that old

Erwin and his sons and daughter had lived here.
He showed us master-builder drawings he said
were likely from the hands of three generations
of von Steinbachs who shaped the Cathedral.
We saw the originals of the statues
of "The Church" and "The Synagogue," the lion-cubs
from the old central doorway gable.

It was a good thing, the guide said, that the *copies*
were outside since wars and revolutions
had ravaged the exterior for centuries.
When everything that mattered had its closing
time we wandered back into the Christmas
streets and past the market stalls, down *rue Brulée*
where long ago they burned the Jews some said

had poisoned the city's wells. We wandered
over bridges and canals, and crossed the Ill,
the river that shaped the islands, and found ourselves
in some small bistro in the *Petite France* district.
The first thing she said over dinner was this:
"I don't think that guide believed the Sabina
stories." "That's his problem." "Yes, not ours."

We had a pack full of pamphlets and books
in English, French, and German about Strasbourg
and the Cathedral that we'd bought in book shops
on our lunch break and though it was against
our usual code of not reading while eating
we were hungry for more knowledge and lore
about Our Cathedral and old Erwin and Sabina

and besides the *choucroute garni* with strong
bistro mustard on the crusty peasant bread
and the large crocks of Mützig our favorite
nectar of Alsace the best beer in the world
always perfect on a cold winter night
was a meal that did not demand exegesis
or even close attention so we read in our trove

of homework all through the meal, reading details
to each other now and then, not conversation
but shared scholarship, excited research
that should usually be kept far from food.
"Listen to this," she read: "*The Cathedral spire
points skyward like an admonishing finger.*
Isn't that ridiculous? The writer must be English."

"Yes," I said. "They usually are. Ridiculous."
"Even that fat rude German today who asked
us to take his picture in front of the church
said something better than that. What did he say?"
"*Ziss schpire is a V-2 rocket aimed at heaven.*"
"Yes and you said—" "It's a von Steinbach von Braun
prototype for a space-shot moon-landing."

I ordered two more mugs of Mützig.
"You like Claudel don't you?" she said. "Sometimes."
"This book says he called the Cathedral
*a pinky-red angel hovering over
the city.* That's awful. Angels don't hover.
And *pinky-red* is flat-out terrible."
"It's a bad translation. That poem's OK

in French. And maybe *ange* feels different
if you're French." "So now angels are tribal?"
"No, but language is." "Remember that tourist,
that American in Angers who thought *Angevin*
meant *angel win*e and tried to order some?"
Remembering, we both laughed. "It says here Claudel
evoked the *pulverized light through the stained-glass*

windows. Not bad. Oh no, listen to this—
he calls snowflakes *little angry angels*
stinging the flesh. I'm sorry, you can't say that."
"He didn't. Poetry can't be translated.
Especially not in a tourist brochure."
She looked in the front of the little book.
"It's not a tourist brochure—it's a booklet

about Claudel's poetry published in the 1930s."
"That's another problem. The 30s. And published
in England?" "Yes." I read her some of the things
Goethe said about Steinbach and the Cathedral
and then it was time to go, they wanted to close
the bistro. The *patron* and his wife were very
French and thus very merry in a quiet way

and of course did not say or do anything
to indicate it was late or that we, their last
customers or guests, were keeping them up.
In fact, the *patron* brought us two glasses
of an intensely fruity *marc* that he said
was a homemade plum brandy from his brother's
farm and it was France and we were family

before we said goodnight and went out into
the light snow swirling in the narrow streets
walking fast holding hands singing in the snow
until she said *go away little angry angels*
and we stopped, brushing snow out of our hair,
in the shelter of a closed Christmas Market stall
and watched the dark snow-magic of Our Cathedral.

In our ancient timbered room we spread our books
out on the bed. I got one of the two bottles
of local wine we'd bought that afternoon and I had
put on the windowsill, opened the window
just enough to chill them. "Let's have the Riesling,"
she said, so we did. It was cold and good,
dry, fresh, opulent, mineral and floral,

and because I failed to write down the full name
I only remember that it was a *Ribeauvillé*
Grand Cru and the wine-cave man who praised it
was right and it was perfect for quiet reading
in the warm bed with the curtains on both
windows pulled all the way back so the snow-light
outside became a part of what we were reading.

I went back to the Nietzsche and when I came
to the part where he talked about Goethe
praising Steinbach and the Cathedral
and the *strong rough German soul* I held the book
closer to the light trying to decipher
what Foucault had written in the margin there
and finally asked her if she could make it out

but we couldn't make sense of Foucault's
marginalia and I forgot to ask
him when I returned his book back in Paris.
"Pour me some more of that angel-wine," she said,
"and are you ready to tell me what your Nietzche's
point is because his prose gives me a headache."
"He's not *my* Nietzsche. But this ain't bad stuff.

It's all about the different ways we use
and abuse the past—treating it as monument,
or with antiquarian curiosity,
or with a critical understanding
that might inform the present." "I *read* that part—
seems boring, obvious, German." "He *is* German
though he tried not to be." "But he doesn't

understand what *we* get from the Cathedral.
We're not monumentalizing it,
not antiquarianizing it, not criticizing.
It just *is* and now we're part of what it is."
"Reckon that's what he and Goethe mean when
they say the proper use of the past is to *quicken*
the present." "*Quicken-schmicken,*" she said,

"again obvious and boring. What that Cathedral
does for us destroys all false phases of past,
present, future. More angel-wine, please."
I poured the last of the good Riesling.
"You're right. Time is suspended, destroyed,
transcended. Stone-grace erases gravity.
Art quickens the heart and frees both flesh

and spirit from the ravages of time.
Be-bop-a-lula." I leaned over and kissed
her nose. "*Don't,*" she said, "let's read some more.
Be-bop-a-lula yourself Quentin Compson. Let's have
some more wine and read for a while." "OK."
I went to the window where the snow
was coming in through the crack and the wine

bottle was cold and snow-wet at the bottom.
I opened the wine, rinsed and dried our glasses,
and poured the red wine. Glasses touched, we tasted:
"Ohh that's good and cherry-dark and smokey,"
she said, "it almost tastes like Burgundy.
It's very very far from Germany.
I didn't know they had real red wines here."

"Me neither. It's Pinot Noir. The cave-guy
said it was the best Alsatian Red, said
it comes from *terroir* cultivated by French
Benedictine monks homesick for Burgundy
in the twelfth century." "It's good." We looked
at the label: *Rouge d'Ottrott.* I remember
because we laughed at the rotten name for

a very good wine. We drank it and read.
Finally, she said: "I'm through. I can't keep straight
all these France-Germany changes they all
keep writing about like people in Kentucky
arguing that North-South border state stuff."
"It's simple. Alsace was France before there was
a France; and German long before there was

a Germany. Back and forth always, war-prize,
Free Imperial City of the Holy Roman Empire.
Voltaire said it best: *Alsace is half German,
half French, and totally Iroquois."*
She laughed: "That's pretty good. I'll settle for that."
"Voltaire was sharp and funny when he wasn't
écrasez-ing his thing and paving the way

for the idiots who started to tear down
Our Cathedral on the egalitarian grounds
that its height was politically incorrect excess."
"Sounds like New York and California now.
Shouldn't we turn the light out now?" "Yes."
I turned off the lights and sat on the edge
of the bed drinking the red and watching

her stand at the window in her long old-fashioned
white cotton nightgown, sexier because
you couldn't see through it, even with the snowlight
streaming through her into the dark room from outside.
She stood there a long time looking across
at the Cathedral and then I stood there with her
and we finished the wine. Then we went to bed.

She whispered softly: “I just saw the White Lady.”
We both knew what that meant, had read the stories
of the ghost-lady of the Cathedral.
“She was spiraling upward, whiter than snow
and very beautiful, around the tower
then she disappeared into the stone.
It was Sabina.” “The books don’t say that.”

“Who cares? I know it was her.” In the dark bed,
watching the snow-light pulverized through our
curtainless windows, we heard her voice whisper
as if another voice spoke: “When Erwin
von Steinbach lay on his deathbed he asked
Sabina to draw the curtains back so he could see
his Cathedral’s rose window one last time.

He stared at the Great Rose and then he wept
and whispered *I am ready now* and ceased
to breathe. Sabina, stunned, saw the image
of The Rose imprinted on her dead father’s
eyes. At that very instant, a flock of crows
circling the Cathedral tower vanished,
and a flock of white doves replaced them

as the death knell rang from the tower bells,
not rung by human hands.” We were quiet
a long time, then she said: “You remember
how your father used to talk to me for hours
and tell me everything there near the end?
Why didn’t Daddy tell me about Erwin
von Steinbach and this miracle-cathedral?”

“I don’t know. He never told me much
about it. It was only my people
two and three generations back who talked
at all. He almost never talked about the past.”
“Maybe that’s because—Mr. Great Gatsby—
you never asked him.” “You might be right.”
We held each other tight and then we were asleep.

In the morning, we checked out after coffee,
saluted Our Cathedral again, drove
across the Rhine and into the *Schwarzwald*
to the ancestral village of Steinbach.
We went first to the heroic memorial for old
Erwin, prepared to be moved, but it was very cold
so it was not like Goethe's pilgrimages

to Erwin's grave and we composed no prayers
as Johann Wolfgang did. In the village
bookstore the old curator told us all about
Steinbach, the village and the man. The place
had been the home of stonemasons for a thousand
years and was long famous for its millstones.
He said the Steinbachs were always builders,

stonecutters, for many hundred years,
but they were all gone now. The greatest
of them all was Erwin, supreme artist
of the Middle Ages. And Sabina
was the first great female artist of Europe
and a lesson to us of the power
of extraordinary women in that time.

Then he asked if we knew that Erwin had
been a Knight Templar and after the suppression
he had founded Freemasonry and was the first
Grand Master. He seemed to feel an urgency
in all this that his actual words could not convey.
He talked about Goethe and the Illuminati
and how many worshipful masters of Masonry

from all over Europe were here in this place
for the dedication in 1845
of the Memorial to Erwin and a secret meeting
of the Illuminati. Hands trembling, he showed
us a manuscript in black-letter Gothic
cursive that, he said, described the ceremony
and made cryptic allusions to secret gatherings.

My tired eyes resisted reading the old script
that blurred my vision while he rambled on
about things we had not read in any book.
As usual, Sparrow came to the rescue,
said she was very hungry, could he recommend
a place to eat in the village. He walked
us to the door, pointed down the street,

said that was the best *Gasthaus mit zimmern*.
We went there, ordered beer and lunch, and smiled
at the locals who looked at me the way
they always did at the Lancaster Farmers Market
and in that Pennsy *Strasburg*. They were curious
and friendly but their Black Forest English was not
very good and I was suddenly too tired to speak

or hear in German. When the innkeeper
brought our food, he said: "You look like you haff come
home." When I said our name was Steinbach it seemed
to make him very happy and he told
everybody else in the *stube*. All through lunch
locals came by our table, said things we half
understood. There were *zimmern* upstairs

and I had been thinking maybe we'd spend
the night there. Sparrow whispered: "I know
what you're thinking but can we please please please
go back to France?" "Yes." I paid the bill
and shook hands with some of the locals
and the *Gastwirt* who slapped me on the back
and then we were outside and in our car

headed toward the Vosges, home to Alsace, to France.
"They were nice," Sparrow said, "but they talk
like words are cannonballs and sentences are tanks
they drive right over you." We felt better
when we crossed the Rhine. As if our car were drawn
by some ultimate lodestone we detoured
through the center of Strasbourg and stared

one more time at Our Cathedral before
we started west toward Paris and Sainte-Odile.
We talked about what we'd seen and learned,
and many strange things we'd read and heard.
She said: "Was Goethe wrong or just naïve
about the rise of the Gothic? It's not German,
didn't start here. Didn't he ever *see*

Notre-Dame or Chartres or St.-Denis?"
"I don't know." "Well, please tell him and your old
Nietzsche that Erwin von Steinbach *did*
and he knew what he saw and brought it here."
"OK I'll tell them." "All this strong-soul
Germanizing talk is just so tiresome—
like some of our guides and most of those people

in that Steinbach village. All Teutonic
monumentalizing and Byronic
Lutheranizing, fantasizing,
romanticizing rough strong German souls.
That is not what built Our Cathedral."
"No." "I mean it all starts feeling like one
of those—what do they call those country folk-club

shows we've seen in Bavaria and Austria?"
"*Heimat Abends*?" "Yes those. Stir in some Wagner,
delete the great music, destroy it with caricature,
simmer history and tradition with blended
blood and soil mystiques and we know where it leads.
And it sure as hell never built any Cathedrals."
"No it didn't." "I don't mean to be so hard

on that village and all that heavy talk—it just makes
my head hurt and it's not *our* Erwin, not you, us,
not miracles in singing stone. Will you do me a favor?
Help me forget that village-talk and let's call Erwin by
his French name the rest of the way home."
"*Herve de Pierrefonds*?" "Yes. Make it your pseudonym
for the poem you will write about all this.

How does *Pierrefonds* translate?" "Stone-something.
Stone-background, maybe stone-heart, foundation."
"*Merci Monsieur Pierrefonds*. Now we're Iroquois
again." "You're Cherokee." "Yes, but I was ravaged
or ravished by a warrior from another tribe."
We took the road that led to Mont-Sainte-Odile.
Halfway up the mountain, we stopped at her

sacred vision-healing spring, looked at her
eye-and-book iconography, washed our eyes
in Odile's shady ice-cold spring. Vision cleared,
cleansed of that old Gothic black-letter manuscript,
free from Illuminati and Masonic blur.
We parked at the top of the mountain, toured
the convent, saw Odile's sarcophagus, just

missed a Mass and when it ended a swarm
of pilgrims came out of the church and we
followed them to the pilgrim's restaurant
and lodging quarters. We checked the menu
and the rooms and decided not to stay there:
Odile's Feastday was coming and the place
was too crowded and we had to leave

in the morning and get back to Paris.
We got a warm baguette, wine and *chèvre*
at the shop then followed the trail-marker
signs to the *Mur Païen*, the Pagan Wall.
It was a long walk, and cold, but intense
afternoon sun was melting yesterday's snow.
We came to a section of the mystery-

wall where the great unhewn blocks of stone
put in place thousands of years ago,
prehistoric or Celtic no one knew,
formed a perfect six-foot high table
and we climbed up on the huge stones in the sun
and ate our bread and cheese, looking out and down
over the vineyard-and-village strewn plain

of Alsace. An old man came down the trail,
we all *bonjoured*, he paused to talk, we all
spoke French. He leaned against the Pagan Wall.
Sparrow always kept four communion cups
in her purse, small glasses not plastic, for just
such chance encounters with strangers who might
share wine and words and time: I poured, she handed

him a glass, we all touched glasses and drank.
He was curious—were we pilgrims, where were
we from? We told him. Then he explained the wall,
over ten kilometers long, three meters high
in some places. I said *we are students of stone*
and Sparrow said *we are not tourists, we came*
to Strasbourg to study the Cathedral.

This pleased him immensely and his tales started.
I filled our glasses with wine. He spoke of the man
some call Steinbach we call Herve de Pierrefonds
whose work was the highest art wrought by human
hands. He talked of many things we'd read and some
things not read anywhere. He said *Sabine*
de Pierrefonds came here to Sainte-Odile

with her father in the early 14th century
to pray to Sainte-Odile for healing of an eye
infection she had, stone-dust from her work
on the Cathedral. She prayed, washed her eyes
in the sacred spring. Everything came clear.
In gratitude her father placed the Cathedral
under the eternal protection of Odile,

the Patroness of Alsace, and they both prayed
to her every day thereafter. That was one tale
we'd never read nor heard. Oral tradition, the voice
of the people talking through the veil of lost history,
was always better than occluded books. We bid
the old man, like a pilgrim from another time,
good afternoon and watched him walk along

the ancient wall. With western sun-slant came
the chill and we hurried back along the trail,
crossing the *Sentier-des-Pèlerins*, knowing
we could walk that another time. "We passed
an auberge at the base of the mountain."
"I saw it. Rooms and restaurant. It looked good."
"Let's stay there." We got our car at the convent,

we drove down the mountain and when we reached
the bottom, this time I saw the sign—*OTTROTT*—
and I knew at least the red wine would be good.
I forget the name of the hotel though I think
Ami was in its name but you never forget
a village named Ottrott—very small, some castle
ruins, a few restaurants, bare winter vineyards.

We checked in our chosen place. I wrote our names
in the Livre d'Or: *Herve et Sabine de Pierrefonds.*
The owner looked at the book, smiled, cocked
his head at us. I forgot about the passport drill.
I handed him our passports, he looked at
our names, our pictures, our faces, I pointed
at our last name said *You see? A play on Steinbach—*

pseudonyme, nom de plume. He got it right
away, laughed, said *D'accord. J'ai compris—*
Bienvenue Monsieur et Madame de Pierrebach
et von Steinfonds. We all laughed. I explained
we were writers who loved the Cathedral
and we liked the great builder's French name.
He offered us an apéritif or a glass of wine.

I said *Rouge d'Ottrott* and he pronounced approval
and before we went up to our room with a bottle
of the local *Rouge* we were like old friends
and family. In our room, we had another
glass of wine and it was better than the *Ottrott*
we had the night before in Strasbourg because
now we were there, truly one with the *terroir.*

We went down to dinner in the wood-walled warmth
of the dining room like a hunting lodge
with a bright fire in the fireplace and something
cooking there, turning on a spit. A bell
rang and the owner cranked the clockwork handle
and the *tournebroche* moved again. The aroma
of roasting meat filled the room. The *patron*

came to our table, told us he was also the chef,
and tonight he recommended the *sanglier*,
the *marcassin*, the young boar slow-roasted
on the spit. We started with a *foie gras* salad,
splendid but surpassed by the first taste
of the *sanglier*, the meat so perfect with its
woodsmoke flavor that we only touched once

the currant jelly served with it. The owner/chef
came to our table to be sure we were happy
and describe his desserts but we said the boar
was so sublime we wanted that taste to linger.
He offered us a cognac, came back with three,
sat down with us, we talked about Strasbourg
and Alsace and Paris and America.

Everything was light and lucid again,
we had left Goethe and Nietzsche far behind
in Germany, we were the *von Steinbach Pierrefonds.*
After a second cognac with the *patron* who said
I looked like his cousin, looked Alsatian, and he loved
the stones of Strasbourg as he loved food, we went
to bed. Hike-exhausted we slept safe inside France.

In the morning, after a good breakfast,
I drove and as we went through Sélestat,
where Erasmus studied in the 1500s,
we noted the fine church from the 1100s,
the best Romanesque building we'd seen
in Alsace even if it was somewhat spoiled
by two 19th century towers, what we really

talked about was Pennsylvania and family
history. "Try to remember exactly,"
Sparrow said, "the first time Daddy talked to you
about Steinbach and Strasbourg and what he said."
"I think it was in a letter he wrote to me
when we were in Alabama. Remember?
I had no contact with him for two years

and I wrote to tell him the rare joy
it was giving me to build our log cabin,
especially *the selection of stones to erect*
the perfect sentence of my chimney, a joy
so complete there wasn't any need to write poems.
He wrote back: *Stones are your Strasbourg legacy.*
Maybe you have entered your true Steinbach

heritage, passed down to you not by old tales
told by your grandmother and great-aunts,
but by stone. Do you have red sandstone there?"
"Did you answer that letter?" "I don't think so."
"Do you still have it?" "It was left in the cabin
and lost with everything else when they stole
the tin roof. But I can still see his words

written in bold firm hand, woven like all
his letters into a kind of poem." "Yes," she said,
"Oh his letters: first the weather, then the news
of the world and the Phillies, and then the poem,
the profound thing to hold and keep. Why didn't
you answer?" "I reckon I didn't want to think
about what he said and I know I had

absolutely no conscious sense of any Steinbach
connection with who I was, what I did.
Building that cabin, I was more Dan'l Boone
than anything else." "Yes you were *thoroughly*
the Great Boonegatsby then. And Daddy
understood that because he too had turned his back
on the past and family history and only

wanted to make poetry and song. Just like you.
Why do you reckon he never talked to *me*
about Steinbach, Strasbourg and all that when
we lived there and he talked with me for hours
and days about everything when you were
working, studying, writing?" "I don't know.
I reckon all family histories are surrounded

by a circle of darkness either through
willed secrecy or simple forgetting.
I don't think his dismissal of the past
was the usual simplistic American thing.
Maybe he just talked to you about things
he thought would make you happy. He was
a gentleman." "Was he ever. I miss him.

Why do the best people have to die young?"
The road wound into and through Saint-Dié.
We did not know this stretch of country
and always we learned as we rode, reading
to each other from the best guidebooks
always at hand in the front navigator
shotgun seat. "Listen to this," she exclaimed

(a word that should rarely be used in dialogue
tags but she really did *exclaim, amazed)*:
"It was the printing-press in *this town*—
in *1507*—that first gave the name America
to the New World!" "*Really?* We should have a drink
here." "It's too early to stop. But you're right,
it's a sign, given what we've seen the last few days."

"Baptismal place and seal of America." She had the small
glasses out, popped the cork, poured last night's Ottrott.
I stopped at the end of the street where steps
led up to the cathedral. We touched glasses:
"To America." "To Saint-Dié *godmother of America.*"
The cathedral was there, an indifferent blend
of centuries and styles, but it was red sandstone

and rare morning wine sang in our blood
like the sun on the red stone: *America.*
The rest of the town wasn't much and we
did not need—seeing all the new buildings—
the guidebooks to tell us the Germans
hit it hard, bombarded in the First Great War,
then deliberately destroyed it in 1944

when they were beaten, retreating.
Were they the masters of retreat-destruction?
When you've lost why must you destroy as you run?
Back on the road toward Nancy, Sparrow said:
"You sure that Alabama letter's the first
time Daddy talked about Steinbach?"
I'd been thinking about it for three days

and I remembered something, not a story
he told me, but a story I witnessed.
So I told her: *You know of course I never*
associated my father with manual
labor. He worked in a factory but I never
knew what he did there. I cannot see him
working in the yard, around the house, using

a hammer. His hands were all about the piano.
When we went to the beach he always sat
on the boardwalk, held court with old admirers
from his poet-pianist days who remembered
when he was crowned the Poet Laureate of Atlantic City,
still a teen-ager, and he was known to play the hottest jazz
piano in town. Old fans swarmed around him (once Nucky

stopped, dressed to the hilt, red carnation and all, my father
introduced me) and he never left the boardwalk gathering
places, never came down on the beach even when
my brother and I built the highest most
intricate castles and cathedrals in the sand
and crowds gathered to admire our building craft.
But once I saw his hands work on something

besides the piano. We visited Uncle Sam
and Aunt Maggie who was very upset
that some workmen had destroyed some stonework
in her garden. I watched Uncle Sam's clumsy
effort to restore the stonework with no luck.
I sat there drinking lemonade thinking
I could do it better, watching Uncle Sam's

awkward hands, inarticulate, unversed in stone.
Then, wordless, my father knelt down to the stone—
the only act of labor with his hands
that I can recall—and in nothing flat
his hands restored the stonework, my hands helping,
watching his hands place stones like the intricate
notes and spiraling riffs and runs he played

on the piano. Aunt Maggie—remember?
I told you about her, not really my Aunt
but a second cousin my father said,
later the founder of the Gray Panthers—
applauded, cheered "Bravo master-builder
von Steinbach! He turns the stones and makes them sing!"
Uncle Sam, who looked like the 4th of July

and old posters, cheered too: "Herr Maître Stone-hands
von Steinbach rebuilds the ancient glory!" I loved
the way they talked when I was 10 years old, said strange
new words like Schmalkaldic. *Aunt Maggie was cool-smart,*
elegant-tough, radical-charismatic, and she talked straight
to me about literature and writing as if
I were an adult from the time I was 10

or maybe earlier because I said I was going
to be a writer and she told me she'd been
an English Major in college way back
in the 20s and I could do that too
or just work hard to be a writer and know
that literature, more than any other art,
made the world a better place, made people

better than they are. "Yes, your Aunt Maggie,"
Sparrow said. "I liked her when I saw her on TV
and I like what I've read by and about her.
We should go see her. Where's she live?" "Philly."
"Yes but *where* in Philly?" "Germantown,
of course. At least that's where I visited her
from age 6 to 16 or 5 to 15. And sometimes

they came to our house—mostly Uncle Sam."
"OK let's go see her." "Next time we're in Philly.
She's pretty famous, always busy speaking
everywhere." "So are you." "Yeah right." "No excuses.
If *you* plan it, it will happen." "OK. Anyhow,
I told you that story because it's the first
memory I have of von Steinbach directly

connected with my father and even though
he said nothing that day, what Aunt Maggie
and Uncle Sam said shows it was common
knowledge and maybe part of their usual
discourse with my father—stones and Steinbach
and art—that I never heard." "Let's go see
your Aunt Maggie. Where's your Uncle Sam?"

"I don't know." We had bypassed Nancy, now rode
through war-ravaged Toul. At least, we didn't have
to drive the *Voie Sacrée* again, or go near Verdun.
A straight shot into Paris on the N4. Sparrow said,
reading my mind on Verdun, "Why did the Germans
have to come through here twice in 25 years
and ruin everything?" "The whole world knew

and still knows Paris is the greatest prize."
"That's no reason for them to Germanize
is it? Who do we blame? Luther? Goethe?
Wagner? Nietzsche? Wilhelm? Bismarck? Did they come
here to antiquarianize or monumentalize?
What did Daddy say about the wars?"
"Not much. I just know he hated Hitler.

I actually remember that, his joy on D-Day,
his happiness over the Liberation of Paris.
Earliest things I remember—that and the Bomb
and the Death of Roosevelt. You remember."
"Don't go getting *Ageist* on me. I'll tell your Aunt Maggie.
We didn't know much about the war in the mountains.
Just who was killed fighting in unheard-of-places.

I never heard of the camps until we moved
from the mountains. Did Daddy like the German
writers? I saw all their books in his bookcases."
"I don't really know how much he liked them
but he certainly read them. Said he read
Goethe in German in High School, Hölderlin
and Nietzche too. The only one I *know*

he liked was Heine." "He's the only one I like,"
she said. "At least in that book of translations
of great German poets that we have." "He's good
and besides he chose to live almost half
his life in Paris." "I like him even
better now." "He hated German narrowness,
censorship, brutal rigidity, nationalism, war-mongering.

Saw through that *strong rough German soul* nonsense,
predicted the old baloney Aryan Thor-hammer
would smash all Gothic Cathedrals, foresaw Hitler."
"Wasn't he Jewish?" "Born, yes, then a Protestant
convert. And in his 40s he married
an illiterate teen-aged Parisian shopgirl."
She laughed: "I've seen you looking at those shopgirls."

"Remember when we toured the Kaiser's estate
in Corfu and how the first thing he destroyed
when he bought the place was the statue of Heine?"
"Yes." "When I was a kid Daddy took me
to the Heine Memorial—the Lorelei Fountain
in the Bronx, you've seen it." "Yes, the Rhine-lady
on her river-rock." "He told me then it was intended

for a German park but they would not allow
a Heine statue on German soil. Said he wrote
a poem about it in High School and included
the fact that Heine had a memorial in Paris
but nowhere in Germany. His poem got an *A*,
was published in the newspaper in Atlantic City,
but would have been censored, banned in Germany."

"Those rotten bastards." "When we lived with him
when we first went to Rutgers I did all those
translations for my A+ German course." "I remember—
I loved them all." "Well, Daddy liked my Heine
songs best. Really liked them and was proud.
Said everybody really called old Heinrich *Harry*.
Said he named me after him then we both laughed

thinking of the real name-story." "You don't
have to tell it now, *Rit*." She put her hand
on my knee. "Save it for those who haven't heard it."
"Anyway, he was very happy with my Heine-poems.
Said my streamlined modernist translation of Heine's
most famous line—*Where they burn books, they will
soon burn people*—was better than all the others.

Told me Heine was really more French than German,
and he was happier when I said I wouldn't minor
in German because I preferred the French writers
I was really just discovering then. Remember
after the funeral-shock and what people there
said about his poems and music? I went
to Atlantic City, checked newspaper archives

for old poems of his I didn't already have copies
of, went to his old High School before they
tore it down, checked records, talked to everybody
who looked old enough to have memories of him.
Saw his old report cards, transcripts with all
those A-plusses in German Language and Literature
courses. Then they sent me to Ventnor,

a few blocks from the school, to talk to the old
German teacher, long retired, after teaching
for 50 years. He did not live in a Ventnor
mansion. When I said the name David Stoneback
he smiled, invited me in his tight little
backstreet house. He was very sharp, witty,
90 years old and as fresh as the backbay

breeze that blew across the porch where we talked:
Your father was the best student of German
Literature I had in fifty years. It wasn't just
his gift for poetry, which made his translations
both fluent and acutely lyrical.
He wrote the best student term paper I saw
in fifty years—all about Goethe and Nietzche

and Erwin von Steinbach, the man who made
the Strasbourg Cathedral the miracle
that it is. I carried your father's student
essay with me to Strasbourg and he was right.
I took the train to Philadelphia to show
your father's essay to a friend who taught at Penn.
He immediately said there would be no problem

getting your father a full scholarship at Penn.
That was in the days before Admissions bureaucrats
when faculty had power and rare talent
could be recognized. When I told your father
about Penn he was delighted. But already wed
to his piano and his poetry, he made his choice.
Was I disappointed—yes. But he chose.

I sat there listening to this remarkable
elder who had taught my father for three
full years and, very moved, I said almost
nothing except to answer his questions
about who I was and what I did.
When it was time to go, he walked me to his door,
shook and held my hand. With a slight formal

bow and tears in his eyes he said: *It has given*
me the greatest pleasure to meet the son
of my best and favorite student ever, most assuredly.
I am certain your father was very proud of you.
Stupid in the moved moment, I thought *why does*
he use the past tense, my father was 30 years
younger than him, how does he know he's dead?

Yes, I said, *he lived just long enough to see*
my PhD and first publications.
This is a very good thing, he said. *I regret*
I was ill and could not travel to his funeral.
All of us here who have memory
will remember him as long as memory lasts.
It was quiet in the car for a long time

before I realized she was crying
and then I realized I was too. Finally,
she said: "So that's where Daddy got his
most assuredlys. I always loved it
when he said that. Somehow it made me feel
assured about everything." She dried her eyes.
"You never told me *all* of that before,

not the way you just told it." "Stories are
better told when you're driving, riding through
France, going home to Paris from Strasbourg."
"Oh God I miss him," she said. "I wish he could
hear what his old teacher said, what you just said.
Maybe he heard it all. Thank you for finally
telling it all." "It takes time to tell stories right.

Stories aren't sound bites, like some pseudo-Imagist
poems." "Let's always take time to tell stories.
I hate that new word *sound bite*. Where'd it come from?"
"TV last year? Nixon? Not Cronkite? *The Times*?
Who knows? Who cares? Nothing can be said
in ten seconds: nothing nothing nada."
"If you invent a word people will inhabit it."

"Yes. And it will get worse. Check back on that
in 40 years, say in 2014,
and see if stories are around and if they bite."
"Soon nobody will listen, hear anything
and they won't understand *story* so they won't
be able to tell stories then everything will be dead.
Thank you Mr. Tell-Us-a-Story-Man."

"*Telling* that story *tells* me all I ever
needed to know about why he always took
us to Penn football games at Franklin Field
and what he felt when he sang those great old Penn
songs—{sing}*Drink a Highball at Nightfall*—and why
he wanted me to go to Penn when they wanted me
yet how proud he was I took the path of poetry

and that night he first saw us do a concert.
And it's almost the last story with Steinbach
in it." We were driving through the dreary
industrial landscape of Saint-Dizier.
This was not our favorite part of France and now
it felt like Atlantic City and looked
almost like Camden. "With all his German Lit

and your doing German at Rutgers y'all
never talked more about it?" "I don't think so.
He knew I liked the Modernists and he did, too.
Remember that time he showed us where *The Dial*
was printed in Camden?" "I felt so dumb
I'd never heard of *The Dial.* Duh—*The Waste Land,*
anybody?" "It was OK, you weren't a student

of the 20s, I was, and he was the essence of the 20s."
"And then he showed me that last copy he had
of *The Dial* with Yeats and Eliot, Pound
and Stevens in it, and while you were in class
we read aloud to each other from that issue."
"You never told me that." "He sounded like
a poet should and he just listened when I read,

never corrected me, answered everything I asked,
never forced anything—Oh he was so gentle
and he just wanted to give you his song, all songs.
That's how he gave me *The Dial* and I added it
to the list of things you gave me to be
ironic-Camden-proud about: Walt Whitman,
RCA, radio and victrola, recording sessions

by Jimmie Rodgers, Satchmo, the Carter
Family, Elvis—all of them. Except I was really
proud, no irony. Why'd we leave Philly?"
"Hawai'i. And you forgot Campbell's Soup."
"See what I mean?" "You know he once had a set
of *The Dial*, all the golden issues of the 20s—
everybody in them—and they had rare book

value by the time I was a kid when
he started selling his books and rare records
and rarest stamps from his collection to get
money to take us to Phillies and A's games,
Penn and Temple football games, and Warriors
and Big Five basketball games. And bus trips
somewhere like West Point and Yale and Cornell.

Or buy us all Kohr Brothers Frozen Custard,
the largest size, Planters Peanuts and Taylor's
Pork Roll on the boardwalk. *The Dial's Waste Land*
Issue sold for 30 pieces of pork roll.
"Oh God I loved him." Her eyes were wet again.
"What happened to that last *Dial* issue
he had when I lived there? I think it was 1929.

He had things written in the margins. I wish
I had it." "It wasn't with the books I got—
the best stuff was all gone." "She sold it, or worse,
gave it away to somebody who couldn't read.
I'm sorry, I don't hate her anymore.
And I've almost forgotten how he had to play
his jazz records in the basement because

as he always said *Mommy doesn't like*
my jabby-jooby music. I hated her then."
"Me, too. If she could've moved his piano
she would've banished that to the basement.
Except then she couldn't play her hymns.
Still, jazz and hymns together make a great gift."
"It all depends," she said, "how you wrap

and give the gift. I'll just say this now and maybe
I'll never think of it again. I can't forget the day
he said *You know what Mommy thinks of my jazz*
but do you know she fell in love with me for my
music and my poems and now she doesn't
even like my poetry anymore. Maybe I should've
been a farmer a stonemason an architect—

things that were in my blood. I cried. He cried,
just a little. And I promised him I would
always sing with you wherever your music
took you and you'd always be my favorite poet.
That part of that day I'll never forget."
"You never told me all of that before.
Not the Steinbach part. Not your pact with him."

"France is good for story-telling. Where are we?"
"This is Sézanne coming up." "I thought he
was in Provence." "Not much over 100 K
to Paris. Just north of here is where Foch
whipped the *Boche* in the Battle of the Marne."
"Good," she said. "I'm starved," I said. "How about
some of that bread and pâtè and Morbier?"

We'd picked up some stuff at our last gas stop.
"Do it on the road so we get home before dark?"
"Yes." Trained by France, we would normally find
a picnic bench by a stream but getting home
to Paris was serious business. And it was cold.
We ate for a while without talking. She handed
me a glass of wine. In that country it was OK

to drink and drive. It was good and necessary.
Ah! but that was in another century—
The only time we were ever stopped by a cop
in France he scolded us for drinking inferior
wine while driving. "No more Steinbach tales?"
she said, refilling my glass. "Just a little,
there at the end. The last time we saw him,

when he came to Krum Elbow, he did talk about
stone and Steinbach. He commented on the crude
fool's-gold stonework on the porch pillars.
When I took him for that drive alone in the country—
while you kept her busy getting things ready for dinner—
he noticed most the good stonework, the stone barns,
the gatehouses, the stone walls of the great estates.

At least, he said, *not everybody in this country*
has forgotten the knowledge, the craft of stone.
I told him I had been collecting stones
from all the ruined barns and walls, the good ones,
because I wanted to build things and I loved
the shape and feel, heft and color of every
stone I selected. I told him how I dreamed

of tall chimneys I would build and the next
day I'd see a certain stone from my dream on some
back road ruined gatepost or crumbling wall
and bring it home." "God," she said, "we did that for two
years after you first saw Europe! And when
we get home I won't see you for months because
you'll be working on your three-storey chimney."

"But that last day with him we were still
at Krum Elbow and I hadn't started the great
Tour de West Park yet though I took my stone
collection with me when we moved right after
he died. Remember—then I was building that big
stone grill and BBQ pit out by the garage?"
"Yes, remember I helped you carry the stones."

"Yes. We sat there that day by my drystone work
looking out over the river toward Roosevelt's
place and we talked about family history.
I told you some of it then. First, I asked
him about the stories of the wild Russian
somewhere in the family tree. He said *SShhh*
and gestured with his eyes up toward the porch

where my mother and grandmother were sitting
with you. Then he whispered *That's their side*
of the family and I've told you all I know.
About the stonework here—he reached out
and touched the top stone of my unfinished
grill and pit—*nice stones, good design, clean lines*
but how can you hope to build true when you've

never worked with a master mason, served
no apprenticeship in the craft? It's true
stone is in your blood. Mine too. And my father
and all before him. But the last to really work
in stone was my grandfather. Then we stopped.
My father a Railroad Executive,
me a would-be poet and music-man.

I feel what you feel about stone but the line
was broken long ago. You can't be everything.
Your apprenticeship was to song and poetry
and you are now a Master of your craft—
der Herr Doktor. He laughed because my PhD
had just been conferred and he was proud
to call me Doctor. Then I told him Pete

had stopped by last week when I was working
on the grill, helped me set in place a big stone.
Then Pete said if you want to join the Masons
there'd be no problem at the local lodge.
My father looked at me with raised eyebrows,
said *Why would you do that? Freemasonry*
today has nothing to do with stone. That's why

it's called speculative. But I won't tell
you what and what not to do. I told him it
might be useful literary research,
to know what Faulkner and other writers
who were Masons knew. I said this because
I wanted to know what he knew. It worked.
He stared at the Hudson, like Time, and talked:

Here's some family history: My father,
your grandfather, was a 33rd Degree
Mason, well-connected, socialized with people
like John Wanamaker, a worldwide Masonic
leader, both at their Lodge and at places
like the grand old Union League Club in Philly.
Aunt Maggie and Uncle Sam called them the Illuminati

of Philadelphia and who knows where else?
It's enough for you to know that Stoneback
men were Masons as far back as can be traced,
maybe all the way back to the Knights Templar.
And I was the first to choose not to join
because it was all part of the past I turned
my back on. I know you heard old tales and legends

from your great-aunts and grandmother about
our ancestor Erwin von Steinbach. Maybe
they told you he was a Templar, then the founder
of Freemasonry before it became speculative.
But what does that matter—what he built matters.
All the hocus-pocus symbolism that came later,
the secret handshakes and passwords that would

get you a discount from your local hardware
store, the secret signs of distress that would
get you help supposedly anywhere in the world
all seemed like childish mumbo-jumbo
secret Illuminati conspiracy theory
to me so I turned my back on all of it.
Either you work with stone or you don't.

"You remember—it was at this point you called
down to us from the porch *Y'all come. Dinnertime.*"
"Yes," she said. "So that's what y'all were talking
about so intensely." "Yes. Right before
we climbed the tall steps, he said *I've been told*
about Erwin von Steinbach since I was an infant.
All the stories. I have studied pictures

of the Strasbourg Cathedral since I was a boy.
I planned to make a pilgrimage to Strasbourg
but then the Great Depression happened to us.
I have dreamed that pilgrimage for 50 years
and I know why young Goethe worshipped Steinbach:
and I have tried and mostly failed to translate
that stone-song through my piano and even

my music at its best lasts a few minutes
and our ancestor's stone has lasted 700 years.
And if the barbarians can still be held at bay,
it will last another thousand years.
Promise me this: you will go to Strasbourg
as soon as you can and pay my respects
to our forebear, his vision, his triumph.

If you think of it, take a stone from the old
1680s Stoneback Homestead, from French Creek Falls,
or even from Byron Street or somewhere
in Philly or Atlantic City and place
it on his grave or better yet on the altar
of his great church. I promised as we climbed
the steps then said *But you'll get there soon*

and maybe we can go together. How could
I know, walking up to dinner, it would
be our last conversation and he would be dead
in a few weeks. And if I had known, what might
I have said different. But I think he knew."
"Oh God I miss him. You're not supposed to die
at 60. He could have been there with us yesterday.

You told me most of that before. All except
the stone but that first time I saw you leave
it on the altar. Where was it from?"
"Virginia Avenue, Atlantic City,
his boyhood place where he was happiest."
And then we were home in Paris. We ate
at our local café, looking across the river

at Notre-Dame. After Strasbourg it was small,
domestic, our intimate somehow homely
parish church. In my hand, she placed a stone:
"Red sandstone from near Erwin's Western Wall."

III. Sabina von Steinbach c. 1274–?

Thanks to the bold piety of this woman, Sabina,
who has given me form from this hard stone.

Original rendering of a scroll held by the statue
of St. John the Evangelist at Strasbourg Cathedral
attributed to Sabina von Steinbach

Sabina von Steinbach Sculpting the Figure of 'Synagogue'

Title of Painting
by Moritz von Schwind, 1840

Erwin's daughter, Sabina von Steinbach, sculpted these haunting figures of
'Synagogue' and 'Church' traditionally held to be self-portraits.
She was a master builder and sculptor who took over her father's business
when he died. She created many stunning sculptures here and in other
churches such as Notre-Dame-de-Paris. She was said to be very
beautiful and very disciplined and the first great woman artist of the
Middle Ages. And now some young professors claim she never existed . . .

Tour Guide, Musée de l'Oeuvre Notre-Dame
Strasbourg Cathedral 1988

Some years ago in Eighty-Eight
we made our old detour,
the seventh time we took that route
to hold the dream of Strasbourg.

This time the nuanced color struck us again
for we had just come from Collonges-la-Rouge
the red sandstone village in the *Limousin*,

before that, Roussillon in the Vaucluse,
red ochre village in Petrarchan hills
where we recalled the time our brand new shoes

turned red in the rain on the red sand beaches
of Prince Edward Island and how the road ran
red clay near Alabama cabin and reached

way back to Philadelphia where
first tears had flowed for red
sandstone, and Camden's Christmas Eve
stonesteps all bathed in blood.

Old forms are rarely adequate to hold
the things we feel and never say aloud.
By this trip Erwin and Sabina felt
like members of the family and they were.
But we had never talked about Sparrow's
long ago strange dream of names, before she
ever heard von Steinbach names uttered, or read
a word about them, before I told her
anything about my Strasbourg history.

This was not something easy to talk about:
When she had difficult surgery in the hope
we could have kids, she said before they rolled
her into the operating room: "We'll have a boy
and name him Rittenhouse, call him Rit,
and a girl named Reba after your grandma
and call her Reba Jay." She knew my Grandmother
Reba Stoneback by then and had heard her talk
about my being descended from the Rittenhouses.

But she had never heard or read one word
anywhere about the Strasbourg Steinbachs.
This was still before I had ever mentioned
the Steinbach stuff. When she came out of surgery
the first thing she said when her eyes opened
in the recovery room was this: "We have to change
the names. I dreamed we must call our boy Erwin
and our girl Sabina. Strange old-fashioned names. But it
has to be, I don't know why, how it was in my dream."

"OK," I said back then. When it was clear
the dream would never be, we talked about
it once, and only once, when we first went
to Strasbourg and discovered Sabina.
Sparrow said: "I prayed hard to God for our
Sabina. I wanted her to be a great
sculptor. But I reckon the world can only
hold one Sabina Stoneback every 1,000 years.
So this is *our* Sabina." She touched the stone statue.

"And you'll just have to be the only secret Erwin."
We never discussed again the children
we didn't have, never mentioned, never
a triple bank-shot allusion, but their presence
traveled with us everywhere, instructed us
in the art of loving well the world's lost children.

(As teen-agers, we'd both had three blood-kids
and loved them as fate permitted beyond mere blood.)
Before this trip in '88 we'd read some academic

pseudo-feminist with a radical Marxist anti-Church
agenda—arguing Sabina never existed.
The myth-debunking essay made Sparrow furious.
Real travelers know you should always take
a guided tour (in Europe anyway)
because you never know when you'll get
a Malcolm Miller at some place like Chartres.
We took the next tour and, sure enough, the guide
cited doubts that had recently been raised

as to whether Sabina ever existed.
Sparrow turned and walked away from the group.
I followed her outside. We looked up
at the great tower. She lit a cigarette:
Why should I listen to some kid's stupid
Sabina-is-Dead thesis? There's more evidence
of Sabina's existence than there is proof
that guide exists. "You're right," I said. "Let's see
if the next guide is any better. In 20 minutes."

The next guide told us what we'd always heard
and read, citing Sabina's famous "Church"
and "Synagogue" figures, her work at Notre-Dame
in Paris, her craft and business skills, her
great beauty, then ended with outrage over
the young professors now claiming she never existed.
"If Sabina did not exist," the guide said
chuckling, "we would have to invent her.
The truth is she has invented all of us,

bringing us all to stand together here
in the miraculous *presentness* of her father's
Cathedral that she almost completed."
Everybody applauded the guide and his tips were good.
Over the years, Sabina has haunted
us and followed us, showing up in strange
places. Like Atlantic City. A few years
later we were there when *Trump's Taj Mahal*
had just opened. Aside from our outrage

over how that monstrosity had swallowed
the Boardwalk and stolen the Steel Pier, we learned
that Trump's Folly was built directly over

where my father's boyhood home had stood.
It also sat on top of the old *Silver Dollar Saloon*
site, where my father played his first teenaged
piano gigs. We met an old man at the *Knife & Fork Inn,*
legendary 20s place where my father played for Nucky
and Boss Dock. This man recalled my father playing there,

at the *Silver Dollar*, and other places
that were gone. *Yes, Dave Stoneback. I recall*
one night in '28 your father played
a very long jazzy blues to the tune
of "Corrine, Corrina" only he sang
"Sabine, Sabina"—it went on for many
verses he made up like he was telling
the whole history of the world. When it ended
he took a break and I bought him a drink.

I asked him who Sabina was and he said
"Some famous Medieval Lady-Artist
I'm descended from" and that's all that got
said because right then the gunfire started,
the raiding Feds and the Mob boys firing
back and we ducked behind the piano
and bullets made the strings go crazy zing.
I asked the old man if he remembered
any of my father's world-history words.

Even he probably wouldn't remember--
he made it up as he went along, sticks and stones,
castles and churches, beautiful ladies, broken bones,
wars and revolutions, France and Germany—
a little bit of everything. Why don't you ask him?
"He's been dead a long long time and he never
talked about these things." *I'm sorry to hear*
that son. Nobody tickled the ivory like him.
Hell of a poet too—always read his poems in the papers.

So Sabina strolled the Boardwalk—too bad
she wasn't there to build something for Trump
with taste, made to endure more than five minutes.
A few years later Sabina followed us
to Sun Valley. There was a big Hemingway
Conference and we hosted a poetry reading
and party at our Sun Valley apartment.
Gregory and Ida and some other Hemingways
were there. Usual suspects read poems—Don, Robin, me—

we listened to the local country music station,
sang along, drinks in hand. Then a voice came
loud and clear over the air waves: *This is Captain*
Mack Stoneback with your local crime report.
There wasn't much crime to report and he gave
his name again and said *Come see us in Hailey.*
So when our guests left, we called him, said we'd
be right there and he said he'd wait for us.
We walked into the Hailey Police Station,

introduced ourselves. I said I'd always heard
that all of us who spelled *Stoneback* the way we did
were related. He'd heard that too. His family
had been in Idaho a long time. He didn't know
much history, his father might know more. Did
I want to talk to his Dad? *Yes.* He picked
up the phone, dialed. I watched his hand hold
the phone, a big Masonic ring on his finger.
OK Dad I'll send the wandering Stonebacks right out.

We drove past the Catholic Church where Hemingway
paid for a new roof, paused by Pound's boyhood home,
then drove a pieceways down a country road.
We found the little house right away, saw
the stone wall Captain Mack said we couldn't miss.
The Captain's father was at his stone gate, waiting.
"He looks like a Stoneback," Sparrow said.
We went inside, he gave us ice-cold beers
that we all drank from the longneck bottles.

We talked family history, old Pennsylvania
connections. I knew right away not to expect
any big discoveries when he said:
My people come West with the first Gold Rush.
We'uz jackleg miners and hardscrabblers
ditchdiggers stoneworkers all over the West
long as anybody can remember but the old
people always said we come from Pennsylvania
once. He asked us what we did for a living.

I said I was a writer and we were both singers.
You moo-sicians, too? What's your instrument?
We both play guitar and piano.
He said: *I kin barely write my own name*
and if I'uz to sing the crows'd fall dead
outen the sky. Pie-a-no? All the keys

is Chinese to me. I could see there wasn't
much point in asking him about Erwin
von Steinbach and Alsace and Strasbourg.

Whatever history he had in him was buried
in some inaccessible past, lost in West.
He was a jovial hospitable guy and he brought
us another beer and led us out into his garden.
I'm retired now and all I do is fiddle with rock.
Writers build with words like masons build with stones.
I looked at his hands when he said this, saw
his gold Masonic ring. He showed us fine stonework
in his garden, proud of his wall and terraces,

his fountain and birdbath. Set in his fountain
so the water washed over it and color shone
and shifted in the sun was a pancake-sized
rock, red sandstone. "Is that local stone?" I asked.
No-sir my boy brought that to me from someplace
in France or Germany where he says Stonebacks
come from long ago I can't call the name
but supposedly we all descend from somebody
there long ago named Sabina Steinbach.

I can't vouch for that but my boy's wife—she's
a schoolteacher—found it out in some books.
It's a fact my grandmother's name, and her
grandmother before her, was Sabina.
It was time to go and we walked to his gate.
"Mighty fine stonework in these gateposts," I said.
"Thank you kindly Cousin Stoneback," Sparrow said.
"*Call me Erwin.* Y'all come back y'hear?"
He shook my hand and I think I felt

the secret handshake. I looked at the small
round black stone he put in my hand. "It's local,"
he said. "A good luck piece for you." We drove
away, waving back at him. "Amazing," Sparrow said.
"The signs are all there but they can no longer be read."
"Memory dies but blood and bone still sing and tell."
"Maybe it doesn't matter, Erwin and Sabina
are everywhere." I still have that stone somewhere
in this vast lonesome house with lost stones from many places:

Kentucky, Alabama, Tennessee
Pennsylvania, Havana, Virginia, Gettysburg
Roncevaux, Santiago de Compostela, Puerto Rico

Omaha Beach, Ushant, Paris, Provence
Greece—Delphi and Lesvos and all over Greece—
The Great Wall of China, Shanghai, Suzhou
Australia's Red Centre, Alice and Uluru, Rome, Venice
Hawai'i, Fiji, Tahiti, Panama, Guadeloupe, *Strasburg*
(Lancaster County), Philly, and *Strasbourg.*

I don't know if this poem's about history or stones,
my wife or my father, my spiritual home(s),
my ancient ancestors, my flesh and bone,
or all of the above and everything below.
Now that they are all gone and I am alone
with no one to talk to about these things
except perhaps the lost Lady in White,
Erwin and the holy wind around his spire,
I must go one last time to Strasbourg to sing

Stone and—*

*(Paris & Brittany 1974 / Hudson Valley 2013)***

NOTES

**Note*: Here ends the manuscript bearing the title *The Stones of Strasbourg,* by Herve de Pierrefonds, (which may be an authorial pseudonym that is perhaps explained in the body of the poem).This annotation follows the asterisk in the text: *FINISHED TO THIS POINT.* Thereafter, fragmentary passages are written under the title *The Notebook of Herve de Pierrefonds.* Some of these fragments are here transcribed in the appendix below.

***Note:* All poems in this volume bear the date of composition, with two dates (e.g., 1974/2013) indicating the years that the process of composition began and ended. And since place shapes what is written, for some writers, as much as anything else, the place(s) of composition are indicated. *Additional omitted note*: The Notebook indicates intent to insert a note for the author's Aunt Maggie—Maggie Kuhn (1905-1995), founder of the Gray Panthers and coiner of the term and a great crusader against *Ageism*, entitled her autobiography *No Stone Unturned.*

APPENDIX

From the manuscript *Notebook of Herve de Pierrefonds*: selected passages marked *Related Material: Possible insertions—but where?*

I.

I suggested we fly to Strasbourg and walk up to Saint Odile, or somewhere or other in Alsace.
"I know a girl in Strasbourg who can show us the town," I said.
Ernest Hemingway, *The Sun Also Rises*

Several times between that dark year I spent
in the hospital, too many surgeries
too much anesthesia, too many code-blues,
death's old bastard face my nightly companion

until somehow I rose to wheelchair from
what they called my deathbed, came out the other
side . . . between then and before the day she received
her death sentence that could not be commuted

we talked about going back to Strasbourg
to Sainte Odile. *I wish*, she said, *we could*
return to all the places we have loved
all the places that have loved us and made us

what we are. But there's not enough time, is there?
I know we cannot talk about one of us
going first—true lovers cannot imagine that—
but now that you've come through I know that I'll

be going first: I know I won't be here long.
I'm sure they'll appoint me your Guardian Angel.
I never wanted to be an angel
and I'm glad you never called me that—

we lived so much together in our earth-skin
our heart-and-soul-song rising from blood and bone
I can't think of angelness and lack of flesh.
I'll accept the angel-rank, the Guardian

Commission, but I don't want you to feel
me watching you when your flesh does what it must
do. So when you feel unguarded and alone
know that I'll be on my angel-break in Strasbourg

remember like Hemingway said you know a girl
in Strasbourg who can show you the town
go to Our Cathedral and find me in the night
I'll be with or I might be the Lady in White

soaring around old Erwin and Sabina's
spire, doing the usual Steinbach-ing things—
I might even be up on Sainte Odile's mountain
remember what he said—Monsieur Herve de Pierrefonds . . . .

II.

I can't go with you this trip. Don't forget to ask your
favorite shepherd-girl Countess what her daddy Ezra thought
about Our Cathedral or if he ever wrote anything about
Strasbourg. I'll try to read some Cantos while you're gone.
JAS to HRS 2007

I should have known when she stayed home
and did not make that trip to Brunnenburg Castle
in Italy for our conference-show
on Imagism: Pound, H.D., Aldington

I should have known when I went alone
that she knew things—no self-pity—meant things she said
things like *I know I won't be here long*
things we could not talk about passed over in silence

I should have known the year before
when in the middle of our concert between songs
on-stage she whispered in my ear
I just felt something here I've never felt before

placed both hands like prayer on her breast
and then when the show was over we let it go
she refused to do scans and tests
though now she said more often *I won't be here long*

we wrote that off to fears for dear
friends like Catha Aldington fighting death-by-cancer
in France, unable to appear
at what she called *some dark and dreary haunted castle*

if Catha would go Sparrow would go
but No, I had to make the trip without her
to meet the former shepherdess now
the legendary Countess Mary de Rachewiltz—

Ezra Pound's daughter: I think I asked
the Strasbourg questions but I don't recall answers
because everything was erased
when I got home and they discovered the cancer

that would kill Sparrow all too soon.
Still she fought hard with high spirits and sometimes said
We'll go back to Strasbourg next June
But if we don't promise me you'll write Our Cathedral

and by the way I read some Cantos
while you were gone—please don't Ezra-write our Strasbourg
make it clear and clean like songs in stone
it's true that sweet are the uses of insanity

but I prefer sermons in stones
and books like running brooks and thousand-tongued trees
I'm named for the Forest of Arden
(Ardennes too)— trust me I know when it's too cold for toads

Ez tried, he tried, he tried to write
Paradise and that wind in his last Canto
is what's left of his Holy Spirit
his old once-a-Presbyterian-always-a-doomed

holy haunted ghost but please don't make
our Strasbourg that way find a form or let it find you
make it more than certain Canto tics
and knee-jerk history's sloppy sprawl sometimes stumbling

into sublimity—I'm sorry:
he knew the stone-sublime and sins Contra Naturam
but not for our song—please don't borrow
but break the Poundameter, that is the last heave

sweet are the uses of vanity
pull it up pull it down pull it off how you can
when you set our roads of France
and make our Strasbourg live forever and again

I was impressed with what she'd read
while I was gone and it wasn't morphine talking yet.
And then she looked at me and said:
While you were gone old Dave called from the West Coast

said he's through with poems, back to songs
said what were you doing in Italy talking
about Imagism so long
when you should be writing about our old music

should be making our Songbook
said Imagism sold 200 books and Sun Records
sold 22,000,000 songs
said remind you EP stood for Elvis Presley

not Ezra Pound, said Jerry Lee
and Elvis, Carl Perkins, Orbison and Cash
matter more than Aldington, H.D.
and all the rest, said Memphis was our London

and Nashville was our Paris
said no plums or wheelbarrows on our Metro
said you could flat-out write bareass
rockabilly better than Taras Bulba I'm just

telling you what he said—he knew
you'd know what he meant and only you could do it
so maybe you should write that too
after our Strasbourg but please please please write Sabina

and Erwin first: find lovely lines
like EP sometimes does but make it all cohere
come clear so readers can find
and feel the song they'll someday understand and sing

I won't be here long enough to see
either book but promise me you'll do both—maybe
Guardian Angels can somehow read
at least I know they can sing when they fly away

We never got back to Strasbourg
and some verse moves hearse-slow, buried books like funerals
and . . .
{here this Herve de Pierrefonds notebook passage ends}

OTHER POEMS

The First Lady of the Organ:
A Song, a Kiss for Diane Bish

Perhaps this poem should have a warning label:
If you have the kind of ear that when you hear
the name of the famous press *New Directions*
it sounds to you like Nude Erections;

if someone mentions your erratic style
and you think they praise your erotic flare;
then as you enter this poem please beware—
this is a heart-healthy gluten-and-fat-free poem.

I hate to disappoint you—it's about art not sex.
I'm here to sing the praise of the woman known
as *The First Lady of the Organ*, the world's
most famous organist, with the longest

running TV show in history: *The Joy*
of Music, where Diane Bish travels far
to play the world's great organs. And I still hear
how she played for me long ago and far away.

We were freshmen at a small church college
in Kentucky. She played the best organ
and I was called the best writer in the school.
We were both one in a thousand—*big deal.*

Do the math: if you're one in a thousand
then out of every million all you are
is one of the thousand best. That won't take
you very far. Anyway, we talked about art

when we talked, about what it took to be
a great artist. One day Diane said: "We are
the only two in this school who will amount
to anything." I knew exactly what she meant—

we believed in Art, while all around us
our classmates drowned in desire and lust
and tawdry dreams of what they called success.
One day she said: "Love God with all your heart

and do what you will, what *we* must." I'd never
heard before that Augustinian variation.
All the preachers I'd heard, mostly puritan,
seemed to say *Fear God and be careful what you do.*

Her saying was compelling, promised freedom,
but I did not know then how to love God.
Besides, this is what we said in most discussions:
Love Art with all your heart—create what you must.

But then maybe God is the same thing as Art
and I did not know it yet. One day we sat
alone in the organ loft of the chapel.
I watched her hands and feet move in a way

I'd never seen: she made me hear in hymns
things I'd never heard before. I never liked
organ music before that day. It all seemed just
funeral-parlor-phantom-of-the-opera stuff.

I did not know yet that great cathedrals
were built to hold the sound of great organs
well and truly played. That day we sang a hymn
she made sound like Mozart: I cannot recall its name.

She made me try the organ. I made some sounds
that were not joyful noise. She silently forbore,
she knew my country rockabilly guitar,
my Fats Domino and showoff gospel piano

style. She must have thought I was a barbarian,
musically speaking. In our comradeship in Art,
I was the writer, she was the musician.
She leaned over from behind me, placed her hand

on top of mine, guided me from a C triad
to an A-flat. I might as well say this straight—
I find it very sexy when a woman
leans against you, her hands on top of your hands

moving on the keys. But this was different.
With her, unlike other girls I was alone
with in those days, I did not want to kiss
her, so it must have been about Art's atoning

power. That was when she said: *If we kissed just once*
we'd never make what we're destined to create.
After that we were never alone
in the organ loft again. She spent all free days

and nights perfecting her craft, deepening her art.
I spent too much time on girls, on sports,
on climbing cliffs, cave-exploring, river-diving,
when I should have been reading and writing.

If she made a Gothic Cathedral to stand
a thousand years in the sound of her Art,
I made skinny skyscrapers in an earthquake,
trembling like trees. I flew down-court on fast breaks,

loving the sound of fans proclaiming my name,
the cheerleader chants, the moment of fame
and glory in the noise of the games she never
came to because she had to practice. If every

jump-shot had been a sonnet, every free-throw
a haiku, every river-cliff freefall
an epic, then by now I'd be Poet Laureate.
The kiss of action made it hard to create.

Then I went steady with the cheerleader captain
and everybody thought we would be married.
Maybe Diane had a friend but I think of her
as wed to Art. We always smiled when we passed

on campus, in the sure and secret knowledge
that we were the only ones who'd ever make
Art, create sacred space and time adequate
for what she called the Glory of God and the human spirit.

Sometimes I sat alone in the deserted chapel
and listened to her practice. She never knew
I was there. Her playing turned the building
inside out, upside down, brought Nature folding

in and maybe God leaned down to listen near,
as distant hills came closer, the river ran
backwards and all the creeks flowed back to sources.
Her playing subsumed all mysteries of sound as force.

One day she said she aimed to play in all
the great cathedrals of the world: Strasbourg,
Chartres, Notre-Dame she named, and smaller
churches that had celebrated organs.

We went to the library and she showed
me a picture-book of great cathedrals, said
I will make music in these places, songs like stones
that built these places. You must do the same with words.

I lost track of her after our sophomore year.
I was expelled from college, joined the Marines.
Still seduced by action, I followed dark roads.
Once, years later, I heard vague rumors Diane

had gone to Paris to study with Nadia
Boulanger. Even then I understood
what that meant and knew she was not baking bread
in a *boulangerie*. Then I forgot her completely.

By the time I first lived in Paris, teaching
at the university, having learned at last
the discipline of writing, working on a book-length
poem, my weekly retreat and release

from words and the incessant search for *le mot juste*
was the free Sunday afternoon organ recital
at Notre-Dame. Maybe like Hemingway
I believed it was bad luck to write on Sunday.

On gray Sunday afternoons all through that first
winter in Paris I heard the world's greatest
organists play one of the greatest organs
in my favorite building on this earth.

I heard Olivier Messiaen
play, saw the structural colors of his chords,
perceived his form and rhythmic nuance
in the architecture of Notre-Dame,

heard his birdsong as time and the end of time,
felt his faith—all joy, love, redemption
dancing in Rose Windows and Cathedral stone.
I heard Pierre Cochereau play often.

And visiting organists from far corners
of the earth who came to play, big names
I never knew because I arrived late
from the Brasserie and the concert programs

were all gone from the stand by the holy water
font. One afternoon, I heard an organist
improvise and deconstruct the world, earthquake
of tsunami-sound painting the Apocalypse,

destroying space and place, beyond all time,
ending in a hymn of love sublime.
The Frenchwoman who sat next to me said
the piece was called *Hommage: St. Thomas Aquinas*

but I never learned who the organist
was. Maybe Cochereau or Messiaen.
The piece was called an *Improvisation*.
Around that time I heard someone play

a concert piece that reminded me at first
of Virgil Thomson and his variations on hymns.
I could see old Virgil, how he looked when
I interviewed him at the Chelsea Hotel

about his aborted opera from Faulkner's
Wild Palms. Then the organ hymns left Virgil
behind, went somewhere else. Miracle keys
became testimony to the redeeming sway

of God and Love and Art. That music haunted
me for days and then I learned it was Diane
Bish who played that week. I wished I had known,
I would have sought her out, bought her dinner,

talked about old days in Kentucky in the heart
of wintry Paris. Then I knew she'd kept her vow,
mastered her art and achieved her fame.
Our old talk, our secret knowledge—it all came

back to me like a reproach for the time
I wasted on travel and other diversions.
But it was fun to sing on islands in the sun,
so much fun to be alive. I forgot her again.

I never watched much TV, did not have cable
until recently when the wheelchair claimed me.
I was in my study writing after midnight.
The TV was on some random channel,

in the kitchen, and then I heard *her sound.*
I wheeled fast to the other room and there
she was: Diane playing the organ in some
Cathedral in Germany. I'd never heard

she had her own TV show, *The Joy of Music*,
which blows away *Law and Order* and *Gunsmoke*
for endurance. She looked almost the same
as she did when I last saw her, fifty years ago.

Her dresses more elegant now, her shoes—
(you always notice the shoes of organists).
Those lightning hallowed hands that I once held.
Her stylish hats and capes, as the camera

followed her walking in the sun and snow
in France or Germany or Austria
and she gave TV viewers concise history lessons
about the place and the church where she was going

to play this or that famous organ.
Her special holiday shows could make you
believe in Christmas again—or cry trying
then all doubt vanished in the sound of her playing.

I began to check for concerts at a time
and place where I could go. Last week I heard
she's playing a Benefit for the Arts at Yale.
I googled the event, read about her hymn

improvisations that *blast the crowds out*
of their seats (according to *The Boston Globe*),
read about the *dazzling virtuoso*
performance of the most important classical

organist alive today. The Yale chapel
where she will play must have a great organ.
The picture of the chapel reminds me
of that chapel long ago in the South where she

played for me alone. Maybe it doesn't matter
that required chapel ended at Yale in 1926,
and it's still required at our Kentucky place.
But it takes a place like that to truly shape

enduring vows and visions of God and Art.
Clearly, I'll have to go to Yale next week,
though I swore never to go again, when
they slighted Red Warren and Cleanth Brooks.

I'll have to see if she remembers our old talk
of Art in Kentucky fifty years ago.
I'll go backstage, give her a rose and this poem.
Tell her that I always knew where she would go.

And maybe, now that she is where she is
(and I've somehow managed to write 30 books),
maybe at last, for Art's sake, I can risk a kiss,
another hymn, a song for Diane Bish.

(Wilmore, Kentucky 2013)

Old Man on Footbridge behind Notre-Dame

For Baudelaire always there

On the footbridge behind Notre-Dame,
the crossing to the Île Saint-Louis,
I stopped several nights on the way home
to listen to Stefan the *accordéoniste*

play his tunes above the Seine. He played old
folksongs as well as Mozart, Dvorak,
Smetana. They said he was the last of the real old *Par-ee*,
the last *bal musette* man—his accordion made the river rock.

The first night I put a large tip in his case
and he tried to refuse, saying it was too much.
But I explained I started life as a streetsinger
and all troubadours owed this to each

other. The second night the crowd was thin
so we talked about life and our memories
of making music in the streets. *Without song*,
he said, *memory is a form of suffering.*

I can go days without food but not without
song. Only music fathoms the sky.
Song makes everything allegory.
We talked late. When he left I wheel-walked the long

slow way home around the island. I paused
to admire, as always, the shimmering
bateau-mouche leaf-light on facades of old mansions,
and the downspouts of the Hôtel Lauzun.

All week, after the lectures and poetry readings,
the concerts and museums, attempts to identify
what Sabina carved at Notre-Dame, I stopped to listen
to Stefan: he became my Old Music Man on the Bridge.

The last night, as I was thinking we could fix
the financial crisis if they sold Greece
to China, and maybe they could make
Plato or Aristotle-Land, a vast theme park,

and share the profits, Stefan started doing Piaf.
The crowd, rapt, intense, sang along low, soft.
I sat next to Stefan, facing the circle,
watching the faces, lips, of young Parisians

and tourists to see if they knew the sacred words.
Some did. We sang the Piaf repertoire
that lent itself to *bal musette* accordion,
beginning with *L'Accordéoniste*

including Stefan's patter about the end
of everything, the end of music
when the Germans took Paris. He introduced
me to the crowd as a famous writer who had once

been a legendary streetsinger—that's what *he* said—
and asked me to sing one. He said some of the Piaf
songs I named were not right for his accordion,
but he held the chords low as I sang, *doucement*,

"Non, je ne regrette rien"—then he fired up
his instrument, looking in my eyes,
shouting "*CHANTEZ*, *Chantez*!" so I belted
it out: *Que sera, sera, whatever will be, will be . . .*

Everyone crossing the bridge to the heart of Paris
stopped and many joined in as Stefan played
and I sang loud, over and over:
Que sera, sera, whatever will be, will be

The future's not ours to see, que sera sera.
My friend, the blonde from Berlin who came to visit me,
leaned against the bridge-railing looking like
a blonde from Berlin. But she did not sing

though the crowd sang along in several languages:
When I was just a little boy I asked my mother
what will I be and Stefan's accordion
made the Seine rise up and we all soared

above Notre-Dame. The song lasted ten
minutes and a lifetime: *Que Sera Sera!*
After the shower of coins and bills filled his case
and the crowd departed, late, quiet on the bridge,

he said *let's do one more just for us.*
When I said "Lili Marlene." He said *they*—
gesturing with his eyes toward the world's most
elegant homes and apartments—*they do not like*

German songs. We talked about Marlene Dietrich,
Hero of the French Resistance, but he said
they would throw him off the bridge if he played
a German song. (This, in October *2011*!).

Still, on the deserted bridge after midnight-
quitting-time, he played it, in a susurrant
whisper over the river and I sang it like a secret.
The blonde sang nothing. Then the Old Man

of the Bridge filled his pockets with the Euros
from his case and packed up his accordion.
He said: *This is the best night I've had in years.*
This is more money than I made all summer.

He smiled at me, we embraced, he said:
I guess an old writer in a wheelchair
with a Santa Claus face and beard, a wise old voice
bigger than Father Christmas, is good for commerce.

We thanked each other, shook hands goodnight. I watched
him walk away toward whatever *Rive Gauche*
hovel he called home. Then I realized
he was probably ten years *younger* than me.

But as long as the song endured
we were both still twelve years old.
So I rolled toward home, my elegant apartment
on the Île Saint-Louis, with my friend

the unsingingly world-weary blonde
from Berlin, jaded and melancholy
in her 20s, and she wasn't really there.
I saw she was never anywhere. And I didn't care.

A young local boy came up from the Seine,
offered us a fish he'd just caught. She shuddered.
I smiled and thought of boys on the bridge in *Par-ee*
and sang to the river *whatever will be, will be . . .*

(Paris & Venice October 2011)

Censer and Censorium: A 72nd Birthday Poem

For Johann Wolfgang von Goethe

So Goethe hated tobacco smoke, garlic, and the Cross?
In this he is like all Puritans, lost,
and as such he belongs on any list of things to be disliked

since garlic and tobacco are earth-blessings
to be cherished and many Crossings
give us our best songs and art and somehow heart.

What was the fourth thing Goethe said he detested—
oh yeah, bugs. Who really likes bugs?
We are all brothers in something I guess.

When I was 14, allowed to skip class and read in the school
library, I stormed *Young Werther's drang*-angst, wrote my foolish
young sorrow-novel, junked it, added to my list of things to detest:

Phoniness. Romantic suicide, written or tried, is Narcissicide or
Deicide, God-killing self-loving-hating adolescent mirror-smashing
no true contact with the ostensible source of anguish and sorrow.

When I was in the ninth grade I was fond of words like *putative,*
ostensible, Deicide, and above all I sought a way to live
truly and authentically that would banish all phoniness.

Why has Goethe always felt so foreign and faithless and phoney
and Baudelaire so close and faithful and homely?
Something to do with the Panzer-look and smell of stinkbugs?

At 72, wife gone, Goethe fell in love, 17-tear-old Baroness Ulrike,
proposed marriage via third party. Gutless Goethe, ask her your-
self. How sad that to sustain her interest in your rocks,

your cherished collection of stones, you lined
the box with chocolates for her to find.
At least old Papa Hemingway asked his teen-aged

Venetian Countess (and one other) to marry him—directly, boldly.
Now that I'm turning 72, wife gone, I don't fool with girls under 25
but I speak direct when I write love-letters to all my 25-30-year old

friends and I do not want to marry them all. At least, I hope
this summer's plague of cicadas has scattered the stinkbugs.
Happy Birthday—I still live at the Cross Roads of garlic and smoke

and today after I killed the last grotesque stinkbug
hiding under the mattress in my guest bedroom, the rank odd smell
lingering on fingers, I tried to reread Goethe's *Marienbad Elegy.*

But as always on my birthday which is Bastille Day—
(something about liberty, freedom and terror)—some garlic curing
in my garden needed harvest. Terror and prayer are thurible-curable,

so I lit my pipe, chewed garlic, and e-mailed wide-ranging
young lady friends from Venice to Prague, New York to Kentucky
—messages exchanged *rich in blessings richer still in danger*

from the vast Sensorium, the steely Censorium beyond censure.
That year in Marienbad—it was *1984* after I'd given a lecture
and we'd done a concert at the American Embassy in Prague—

once a place of magic forests and springs and elegant ferns
now sunk in unbearable dread and dreariness,
an old Czech noon-drunk on the street in front of a porn

shop talked about his sad town Marienbad, the glory that was gone,
told me his version of old Goethe and young Ulrike's story there—
somehow different from what I'd read when I was 14.

In that world it was always as if no one had heard anything
and all the voices always said nothing.
In a lover's world things feel truly heard and said.

Love has no truck with understanding (which may come soon).
Love seeks beauty, youth, age, wit, caprice, chocolates among stones,
song, authority, old illusions of innocence, young illusions of wisdom.

Passion must precede understanding. Light your pipe, old man,
elevate swollen ankles, write your Countess, your young lovers.
It's your born-again birthday. Old Goethe is your half-brother.

(Hudson Valley 14 July 2013)

Marine Corps Forced March Mail-Call

50-mile forced march through rain-dripping woods
 a break sergeant says *Smoking lamp is lit*
  kid marine who doesn't smoke waits to hear

his name *mail-call* he holds the hand-written
 envelope in his hand studies postmark
  waits to open it watches rain run ink

bone-chill January woods getting dark
 then pretends to wipe rain from lips their old
  rite kiss the S.W.A.K. on the back

with tough boy-marines a thing best not told
 cold fingers unseal dripping lip-kissed flap
  unfold slow familiar stationery

a letter handwritten letter a map
 of surreal rain-terrain curve and slant
  of her script like curve of her lips her legs

a letter bone-zero rain-soaked descant
 her hand known like her swollen belly-womb
  breasts when AWOL he saw her that last time

after that all-night train ride at that Home
 then the return and his time in the Brig
  and now this handwritten letter ink-run

in rain *it's a boy healthy strong and big*
 they let me hold him ten minutes before
  they took him away O how I love you

(in this age now when no one reads anymore
 handwritten love letters in the rain how
  can lovers know the ones they mean to love)

half-century ago boy-Marine folds slow
 the letter the curve of her flesh places
  it in his pocket *Smoking lamp is out*

the sergeant appoints him to call cadence
 boy takes his place front-right of platoon
  sings *semper why* song *left right left right left*

I don't know but I've been told the old tune
 night-hump *under full load* march into the swamp
  at late last light he sees a cottonmouth

in wet muck by side of stone-free sand-damp
  trail   thinking *it's only rain it will stop*
    he sings recon cadence into the night

he keeps his platoon marching   to dropping
  point   at last he calls a smoking break   goes
    into the wet woods   relieves himself   smells

what must be moccasins   and he knows
  it's not a gator he hears   somewhere near
    in the dark   kneels down   scoops stone-less muck-hole

buries letter deep   where it will disappear
  inters the record of man's lineage
    under dark cathedral trees   eats ration

some kind of Gerber's baby-food canned spinach
  20 miles to go   resumes his cadence-call
    rifle   pack   back-heavy   he chants *left right left*

(Camp Lejeune 1962/2015)

In Places Where Our Fathers Played

For a reading at the Swan Bar: Montparnasse 2012

We all should play in places where our fathers played
And sang their songs and poems in clubs, on stages
My father sang and played jazz piano
A 1920s legend in clubs of Philly
And the speakeasies of Atlantic City

We all should play in places where our fathers played
Keep their songs alive as time recedes and memory fades
My father was also called the Poet Laureate
Of the Jersey Shore, the Atlantic City Boardwalk
He talked of going to write, to play in Paris

We also should play in places where our fathers dreamed
Of playing—the only way that history is redeemed
The Great Depression and then that war
Held him on the homefront, impoverished stillness
Haunted his all-too-brief final years

We all should long to play in places where our fathers
Never got to go, and give their songs to far-others
Before he died so suddenly and young
My father was happy I soon would live in Paris
The last words he said to me: "Sing your song"

And so I played in places where my father never played
Where he only longed to go and finally never made
When I played the clubs of Paris and read poems
Around the town, long ago, I saw him coming home
From the factory, weary, but he always played

And so I played my music, read my poems in Paris
And thought of him home from the factory, unembarrassed
Still writing poems, playing the piano
Every evening after dinner: things fell apart
But to the very end he had his art

And did I see his ghost and hear his ivory kiss
That night in '73 when I played Montparnasse?
Song heals wounds and poems tame the rage of loss
And now that I'm much older than my old man
Ever got to be: I'm here at the Swan Bar, Paris

And he is here with me in a place he never played
His old songs echo, his hands dance, ivory-slide glissade
A boy, watching his father play, like God home
from the filthy factory, then father reads his latest poem
published in the newspaper Poet's Corner

We all should play in places where our fathers never played
Hear mystic solitary voices reverberate—

(Paris 2012)

Angels Do Not Purr & Poems Go BRRrrr

Rub your hands together like this—it feels good.
Directive to poetry reading audience

The other night when it was 12-Below-Zero
my cat in bed in my face and all I could hear
was the sound of her purr filling the dark cold void
of this uniwinterverse, rock of rhythmic noise
warmer than blankets, the roll of her *ronronner*—
(the word for *purr* in French, the thing that French cats say)—

I thought how Pound and Yeats purred, hummed when they composed
poems but I don't go to bed with them for repose
some say bears and squirrels purr, gorillas, elephants
lions and snow-leopards do the mystic voice-dance
but I've never been to bed with any of them
dreaming tonal buzz of joy, dark night of holy hymns

O the experts all agree—purring starts in the brain
signals sent to voice by neural oscillations
strong harmonics of voice-box, steady frequencies
of 20 vibrations per second, piquancy
that heals and counteracts loss of bone density
and other chill effects of zero gravity

They even say that purring's good for astronauts
and that makes me think of Guardian Angels and what
if anything they purr: But No, *sans* flesh and bone
no blood to freeze, Angels do not purr: Monotone
chants of the spirit their only song, incarnation
beyond their ken, their poems all sing salvation

But world-body poems and hymns should not mean but BRRrrr
make flesh and blood and bone feel non-angelic purr
cat-fur and tail-switch, something to touch on cold nights
something to hold in the dark, something you can write—
A poem that has the feel of winter weather
that makes you need, like this, to rub your hands together.

(Hudson Valley February 2015)

MORE ON RECENT BOOKS BY H. R. STONEBACK

About *Homage: A Letter to Robert Penn Warren*

"The poem is a delight, a great read, a rumble of energy all the way through…the rhythmic roll and strut. and the details of the lives braided together."

—Dave Smith, poet, Coleman Professor of Poetry, Johns Hopkins U., past editor *The Southern Review*

"I was blown away by the art and power of the thing…what an intertextual tour de force it is!"

—William Bedford Clark, poet, Editor of 6-volume Warren Correspondence Project

About *Why Athletes Prefer Cheerleaders*

"H. R. Stoneback's recent collection, *Why Athletes Prefer Cheerleaders,* is a singular experience. Every one of these poems epitomizes Pound's old modernist maxim—that poetry should be at least as well written as prose. Drawn together from over fifty years of writing, the book is not only a great gathering of poems about sport; it's a deep sampling of Stoneback's voice. Basketball, baseball, zellball, swimming, diving, walking, fishing, boules—sure, you will find all these sports (and more) invoked. But there's something else going on here too:

Down the great winds at work over the roofs of the land

Down the singing maze of the horror of living

Down the wringing wrists of the honor of living

Down the winding abyss... ("Fast Break")

These are poems rapt by the mysteries of courtside chants and yellowing scorecards, the glories of place and travel. From "In Those Same Sad Old Churches in Camden" and "Marrowbone Creek: Sunday Noon" (written in the early 1960s) to the strange twenty-first-century country of Australia, New Zealand, and Tahiti, you will hear one man's voice telling the holy and broken story of what it has meant to live in the body, in place, in time. There is nothing like it."

—Alex Shakespeare, poet and scholar, Skidmore College

About *Amazing-Grace-Wheelchair-Jumpshot-Jesus-Love-Poems*

"What I love about Stoneback's poetry is that it makes you love poetry…He's a bard, celebratory and rhythmical, with an unmistakable voice and he gets and begets the numinous nature of poiesis."

—Allen Josephs, writer, University of West Florida

"[Stoneback is a] Postmodern modernist extraordinaire!"

—John R. O. Gery, poet, Director Ezra Pound Center for Literature